WILD
ABOUT
Wimbledon

WHERE THE TOWN MEETS THE COUNTRY

To my nephew, Oli, who as I publish is serving in Afghanistan – we are all very proud of him and wish him a speedy and safe return

The map on the end papers is taken from John Rocque's famous *London Map of 1746*.

Contents

Welcome to Wild About Wimbledon

Welcome to my latest book of photographs. Living just across the common in Putney I am very familiar with Wimbledon, as I regularly walk here with my Springer Spaniel, Josie. So it's great fun to be able to share with you some of my favourite haunts. Not that it ends there, as one of the best bits of what I do is discovering new places that I might normally miss if just exercising the dog. She can't always come of course, the schools and the stables for instance but more than you might imagine. One of the things I did discover was how much bigger Wimbledon is than I thought, which has regrettably meant not being able to cover everything. The schools for instance, the Hall and Ursuline in West Wimbledon looked interesting but I just ran out of time and space, so my apologies to them and to some of the others I have missed, nothing personal I assure you.

Over a year in the making, this book has been a massive undertaking and as with projects of this kind many people to thank for their help. Firstly, to Robert Holmes and John Collard of Robert Holmes, Wimbledon's preeminent estate agency, for agreeing to sponsor my book. Robert lives on the common, has a massive stake in what goes on in the world of property locally and is very generous with his support of many local events and charities, so if you are ever in need of an estate agent you know the first place to call. Then there is local historian, Clive Whichelow, who has kindly supplied the introduction to my book and some background on a lot of the places featured. Angela Browne, who introduced us and who is behind the new Wimbledon Way (see page 9). Sally Burrough, a local watercolour artist for her lovely map on page 9. Hopefully, you will have noticed how all the people mentioned so far are locals, something that I felt strongly about. My book is about a community and I wanted as much as possible to gain the help of that community in putting my book together.

Further thanks go to Tim Ball, my new designer, who is only over the park in Kingston. Paul Sherfield, my colour expert, who has been invaluable in getting the most out of my printing. My family, for putting up with the long walks and the late nights. Thanks also to Merton Council, who own much of the area. In the course of a year there are literally hundreds of people I have met and who have helped me and if I haven't mentioned you by name I'm sorry but there is only so much space.

It has been great fun compiling this book and I hope that some of this shines through my photography and that you enjoy my book.

Andrew Wilson
October 2012

Josie, my constant companion, beside the lake in Wimbledon Park.

Wimbledon

A SHORT HISTORY OF THE AREA
by Clive Whichelow

How many Wimbledons do you know? For there are several. To many people around the world Wimbledon means just one thing – tennis. But for those who are lucky enough to live here or nearby it means much more than that.

There is heritage Wimbledon with its blue plaques, listed buildings and historical figures that still live on in street names, statues and monuments. From William Wilberforce to the poet Algernon Swinburne and from Henry VIII to Haile Selassie there are reminders everywhere of Wimbledon's rich and varied heritage that goes back centuries. And beyond this are ancient places such as Caesar's Camp, the iron-age hill fort that housed the very first Wimbledonians over 3000 years ago.

Then there is green Wimbledon with not only the sprawling, 1100-acre Wimbledon Common and the extensive Wimbledon Park, but also the beautiful Cannizaro Park and dozens of other smaller parks, gardens, and pockets of green space dotted around the area that help give Wimbledon its special character.

The common is full of wildlife and has a rich history all of its own including royal visits, duelling, highwaymen and the origins of the FA Cup-winning Wimbledon FC. It can also boast the only remaining hollow-post windmill in the country. Perhaps as a testament to the Common's photogenic qualities it has been used countless times as a setting for TV and film projects. It is also of course the home of the most famous litter collectors in the world!

Which brings us to literary and artistic Wimbledon. The author of Children of the New Forest, Captain Marryat, lived and worked here, as did Georgette Heyer and many other writers. Thackeray was a regular visitor, and the aforementioned Swinburne drank at the Rose & Crown. The sculptor David Wynne lived in the village and even John Constable visited here and completed sketches and watercolours locally. Baden Powell wrote his world-famous *Scouting For Boys* at the windmill and countless other writers and artists have lived here or have been inspired by Wimbledon.

Then there is secret Wimbledon. How many people – even those who have lived here all their lives – have ever seen Wimbledon's oldest house, let alone been inside it? The old Rectory, tucked away behind St Mary's church, dates back to at least 1500 and was very nearly the place where Henry VIII died when he stopped there for the night after being taken ill on a journey back to London. And how many people have been inside the tunnels that ran under Wimbledon manor house? Indeed,

The Old Rectory, the oldest house in Wimbledon as viewed from St Mary's churchyard.

how many people would know where the old manor houses of Wimbledon once stood, for they are all long gone. There are just the hints left in local road names and the Capability Brown landscaped grounds that are now Wimbledon Park.

We should not forget either the Wimbledon That Never Was. Many will remember the old Wimbledon Palais that was not only a venue for some of the biggest dance bands of the 1930s and '40s such as the Ted Heath band or the Oscar Rabin band but also for some of the biggest names of the 1960s including the Beatles, the Stones, the Kinks and the Who. The only problem was that it wasn't in Wimbledon, but in Merton. Similarly, South Wimbledon underground station is in Merton too. On the other hand, it is often said that Nelson's estate was in Merton, but in fact half of it was in the old parish of Wimbledon and some of the road names bear testament to this though the estate, sadly, is long gone. However, the 12th century St Mary's Merton, the church that Nelson attended is still here and proudly displays his funeral hatchments.

For the purposes of this book it is perhaps not wise to define Wimbledon too strictly as bordering areas such as the old parish of Merton were an important part of Wimbledon's story. Not least Merton Priory, which was built in the twelfth century and produced the Statutes of Merton which were an important part of British law until modern times. Much of the priory has gone but the Chapter House remains, as do

parts of the ancient wall. Nearby, in more recent times, were the textile works of both William Morris and Arthur Liberty.

Merton Park borders on Wimbledon and parts of it share the famous SW19 postcode but it is a separate entity in its own right, having been built by the man whose name is familiar to all gardeners, John Innes. This little haven of tranquil tree-lined streets and attractive Arts & Crafts style houses has a history all of its own and was once home to Merton Park film studios which produced, amongst other things, the Edgar Wallace detective films, many of which used the local area, including Wimbledon, for location shooting.

One of the other 'Wimbledons' that should not be forgotten is Sporting

The Polka Theatre, the well-known children's theatre in The Broadway.

If you would like to know more about the history of Wimbledon the Wimbledon Museum in the Ridgway is open most weekends, is staffed by volunteers and relies on visitors' donations. *www.wimbledonmuseum.org.uk*

Wimbledon. Before the tennis started, in 1877, Wimbledon was widely known for the annual shooting event on the common which later transferred to Bisley. It was also one of the first places where rugby was played and it has the second oldest golf club in the country in the London Scottish club based at the windmill. It is also home to one of the oldest running clubs in the country, the Wimbledon Harriers. There are still thriving stables at the Dog & Fox and Swan pubs and the annual Wimbledon Village Fair has horseriding events.

Then there is theatrical Wimbledon. Wimbledon Theatre has been there since 1910 and has played host to everyone from Marlene Dietrich and Laurel and Hardy to Julie Walters and Henry Winkler. To the side of the building is the fringe Studio Theatre (once, the Attic), and just down the Broadway is the well-know children's theatre, The Polka. Until recent times there was open-air theatre every summer in Cannizaro park, and at nearby Merton Abbey Mills is the tiny Colour House Theatre, based in one of Arthur Liberty's old workshops.

So where do all these Wimbledons end? Where do they begin, and where do they overlap? In this book Andrew Wilson gives a good flavour of all the different Wimbledons – perhaps some you have never seen before. But the story doesn't end here because Wimbledon is an evolving story and there is undoubtedly much more to come.

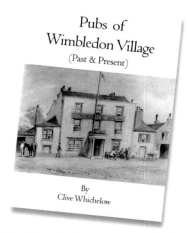

Clive Whichelow has written many books about Wimbledon, one of which is *Pubs of Wimbledon Village*.

Clive.Whichelow@virgin.net

Wimbledon

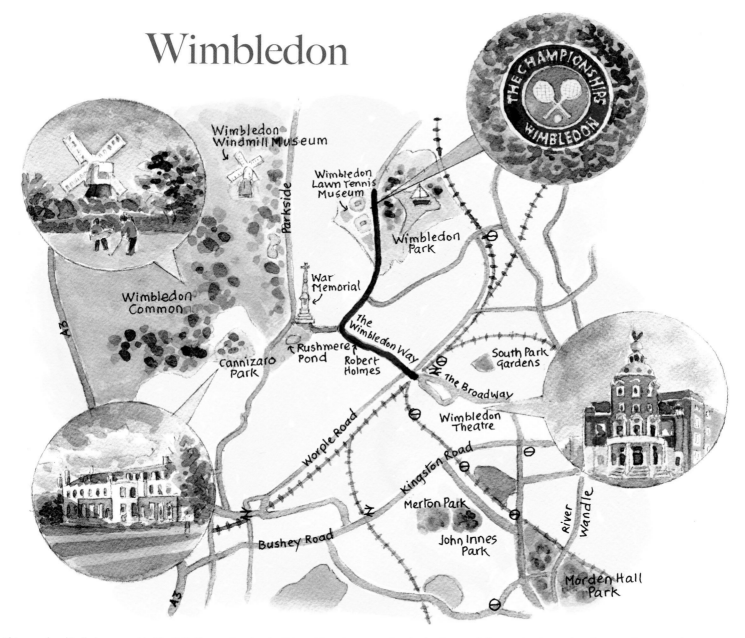

This map has kindly been provided by Sally Burrough, a local artist, and is not meant to be absolutely to scale but to give the reader a fun introduction to the area and some of the places covered in this book. Sally is a local resident and works mainly in watercolours and would love to paint your favourite pet, person or place – please contact Sally at *www.sallyburrough.co.uk*

The Wimbledon Way, as indicated on the map, is a new heritage walk helping people to explore the area from Wimbledon town centre, through Wimbledon Village and on to the All England Lawn Tennis Club, Tennis Museum and the Common. Everyone walking the route will literally walk through some of Wimbledon's fascinating heritage and culture.

Wimbledon has a rich history in its theatres, buildings, transport, people, open spaces and sport.
To find out more visit the website *www.thewimbledonway.org*

The Village

A couple of hundred years ago what is now Wimbledon Village was all there was of Wimbledon. Before the railway came in 1838 it was just fields and farmhouses 'down the hill'. Wimbledon was a desirable place to live even then, being as it was close enough to central London for business purposes but far enough away to be seen as a country village. Many Londoners were impressed by this rural retreat. The writer Thackeray described the common as 'noble' and the air as 'delightfully fresh' and the poet Leigh Hunt was sent here by his doctor for the curative powers of the Wimbledon air. In the 1850s, London was suffering from the 'Great Stink' and it was Wimbledonian Joseph Bazalgette who created the London sewage system to alleviate the problem.

Today, Wimbledon Village is still a much sought-after location combining housing ranging from pretty little mews cottages to the grand mansions round the common with historic pubs, good restaurants, independent shops and interesting walks.

Despite the demands of the modern world the village retains a charm of its own and a villagey feel with horses regularly trotting down the high street from the Village Stables and the bells of St Mary's chiming down Church Road. And somehow, perched on the hill with the common separating it from the urban sprawl of the rest of London it seems to stay in a world of its own.

Previous Page: The old fire station, the building with the clock tower, opened in 1890 and was in use for just a few years before closing in 1907. It is a listed building now containing shops.

This Page: A circular view of Wimbledon Village High Street.

Top Left: View of the High Street from the windows of Holden Harper, Architects. Thank you to partners Richard and Andrew for allowing me to disrupt things for a brief moment to capture this.

Bottom Left: The Gallery in Church Road.

Right: The spur of the High Street leading to Common Southside, past Wimbledon Books.

Left: The Toynbee memorial (just behind the cyclist) was erected in 1868 in memory of Joseph Toynbee, an eminent ear surgeon who founded the Village Club in the Ridgway and was the first to suggest a Wimbledon Museum. The memorial was originally in the middle of the road where the mini-roundabout now is.

Top Right: The Bakery in the Village High Street behind Côte restaurant.

Bottom Right: If you look, the High Street is adorned with these faces, some less pleasing than this one.

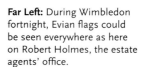

Far Left: During Wimbledon fortnight, Evian flags could be seen everywhere as here on Robert Holmes, the estate agents' office.

Left: The Fire Stables in Church Road was once the Castle pub and the building dates back to the 1820s. Just before the Fire Stables can be found Mint Source (pictured bottom right), a treasure trove for the gift-seeker.

Bottom Left: Dairy Walk, off Church Road, is so named because it led from Earl Spencer's dairy farm to the church. The All England club was later built on part of the farmland. The Walk from Church Road takes you over Marryat Road and on to Burghley Road.

Opposite: The war memorial was built in 1921 to commemorate the men of Wimbledon who had died in the First World War. It was designed by Sir Thomas Jackson who lived at Eagle House in the High Street (see overleaf).

Top Left: Eagle House was built in 1613 by Robert Bell of the East India Company. The extension to the right was added in 1789 by Reverend Thomas Lancaster who ran a school here.

Bottom and Opposite: Winter in the village.

The Olympic Stadium is Sstraight – three metres shorter than Nelson's Column in Trafalgar Square

Above Left: High Street.

Left: Looking towards Church Road from the High Street.

Far Left: Building on the corner of the High Street and the Ridgway.

This Page: During this year of celebration and sporting endeavour, flags have flown and strange signs appeared in the pavements.

WIMBLEDON BOOKS

ROBERT HOLMES & Company

Green Element

Top Left: The Wimbledon Village Bakery has been in use as a bakers for 150 years.

Centre Left: The Village Deli.

Bottom Left:
The Village Florist.

Right: Horses down the High Street are a charming and regular feature of village life (see overleaf for a look at The Village Stables).

The Village Stables

The Wimbledon Village Stables behind the Dog & Fox have been on the present site since 1915 though there have been stables here at the Dog & Fox for hundreds of years. During the 1800s the inn was the terminus for the London stagecoach.

Cannizaro House and Gardens

Cannizaro House and Park were named after Francis Platamone, Count of St Antonio, who later became the Duke of Cannizaro (Sicily). The house is now an extremely popular and successful hotel and the grounds have been a public park since 1948.

Wimbledon Park

As if Wimbledonians weren't lucky enough in having the common nearby, they also have Wimbledon Park. This was literally fit for a lord as it was once part of Earl Spencer's estate. The renowned gardener Capability Brown was commissioned to landscape the grounds in 1765 and created the lake which is still there to this day. When he had finished his work one London newspaper rhapsodised that 'Lord Spencer's place at Wimbledon is perhaps as beautiful as anything near London.' And so it is today.

There were plans to build houses on the land in the early twentieth century but Wimbledon council bought it in 1914 and turned it into a public park. Today there is fishing and boating on the lake, tennis and putting and children's playgrounds in the park, as well as a sports field and the park can be enjoyed by thousands of people every week. The Wimbledon Park Golf Club is at the far side of the lake and here in the centre of an urban area there is a real feeling of tranquillity with the large open skies giving a sense of space and a huge canvas for some spectacular sunsets.

During Wimbledon tennis fortnight the famous queues begin in Wimbledon Park and snake their way through to Church Road, but where else could you queue for a sporting event in such a beautiful setting?

One foggy day in November and the one that didn't get away. The fisherman having rather kindly posed for the camera then slipped his huge catch back into the water.

Formed as part of Earl Spencer's estate, the lake is a major feature of the park, affording spectacular views of the surrounding area, including St Mary's on the Hill.

Previous Page: Summer downpour over the lake.

This Page: The lake at dawn.

Opposite: A Greylag Goose surveying the lake one spring evening.

Left and the Previous Page: the lake at dawn early in July.

Right and Overleaf: Wimbledon Club and Wimbledon Park Golf Club. The Wimbledon Club has been here since 1889 when Wimbledon Cricket Club (established 1854) moved from the common and added tennis courts. It later incorporated Wimbledon Hockey Club and Wimbledon Ladies Hockey Club and also added squash courts to its facilities. Wimbledon Park Golf Club can trace its history back to 1898 and shares this part of the park with the Wimbledon Club.

Opposite: There is always a beautiful display of crocuses in the spring.

Above Left: Sailing is a regular pastime most weekends with clubs for kids during the holidays, where they can try many other water sports including wind-surfing and canoeing.

Top Right: Within the park is a running track, with a beautiful line of Poplars down one side.

The All England Lawn Tennis Club

The All England Lawn Tennis Club has been in Church Road since 1922 and stands on ground that was once part of Earl Spencer's dairy farm. The club had started in Worple Road in 1869 as the All-England Croquet Club and the first tennis championship was held in 1877. This original site in Nursery Road, is now the playing fields for Wimbledon High School.

One sunny evening at the 2012 Championships.

Street Scenes

As mentioned in the introduction to this book, there are many Wimbledons and this is reflected in the varying street scenes around the town and village. Some houses in Wimbledon village go back two or three hundred years or more; Eagle House in the High Street was built circa 1650 and the nearby Rose & Crown pub is of a similar vintage. The town centre has all the modern shops and restaurants you would expect, but in Queen's Road you will find the façades of the old fire station, the Baptist church and the magistrates court in front of modern retail outlets.

Across the road are the new Odeon, Morrisons and other shops with a plaza that often plays host to farmer's markets, street entertainers and suchlike. At South Wimbledon there are still some small independent shops, a modern housing estate and some little Victorian pubs. Some of the street names (Hamilton, Hardy, Victory, etc) remind us that all this land once belonged to Lord Nelson, perhaps our most famous past resident.

The Broadway boasts not only the Edwardian New Wimbledon Theatre, but also the Polka, one of the only children's theatres in the country. And here and there, dotted around the town are Victorian postboxes, old fashioned lampposts, modern statues, and a hundred and one other things that make a very pleasing mix of the old and the new. And just occasionally, there is something really surprising such as the Buddhapadipa Buddhist temple with its winding stream and wooded walks nestling behind a house in Calonne Road. Many Wimbledons indeed.

The Centre

Previous Spread:
The spectacular view you get of the City of London from Marryat Road, see also page 72. Marryat Road is used as part of the route for the fleet of buses serving the Tennis Championships.

Left: The corner of Alwyne Road and Wimbledon Hill Road.

This Page: When the Centre Court shopping centre was built in the 1990s several buildings needed to be pulled down, but it was decided to keep the façades of the fire station, Baptist church and magistrates court (bottom right).

Left: The buildings on the corner of St George's Road and Wimbledon Bridge.

Above: Centre shopping and entertainment.

Strange goings on in the town centre, as part of the country comes to town. Showtime was a free event and part of the London wide arts festival put on to coincide with the London Olympics.

Right: The rather striking stag sculpture, by Isabelle Southwood, found outside Wimbledon Station was erected in 2012 and thematically links the town with the common and also with the stag on Stag Lodge at St Mary's church in Wimbledon Village (see page 84).

Top: The rather beautiful sculpture on the wall of the library and that runs down the side of Compton Road is entitled *Release*, completed in 1995 by sculptor Muhammed Sheibani, an iranian who studied at Wimbledon School of Art. As well as representing the books and shelves of the library, the sculpture also represents the 'physical embodiment of my confinement' (as he spent years as a political prisoner). The red colour also relates to the mountains of his home town, Tabriz.

Above: Wimbledon Library was opened in 1887.

Left: Joseph Ely opened his first store at the corner of Alexandra Road in 1876 and moved to the present site ten years later. The store stayed in the Ely family for over a century but is now part of the Morley's group of stores.

Right: The sundial, found on the building on the corner of Alexandra Road and Wimbledon Hill Road.

Far Right: The pavement signs celebrating the London Olympics found outside Centre Court shopping centre.

The London 2012 Olympic Games will use 26,400 tennis balls, 8,400 shuttlecocks, 2,700 footballs, and 356 pairs of boxing gloves

Right: A Routemaster bus is a rare sight these days, used more for weddings than ferrying passengers about. This one was part of the fleet serving the Tennis Championships.

New Wimbledon Theatre

The angle, and the globe were removed from the top of the theatre during the Second World War as it was felt that they would help German bombers identify the town centre more easily. Most of the theatre's shows however continued throughout the war. The theatre is said to be haunted by two ghosts, one male, one female. The male is thought to be that of Edward Mulholland who opened the theatre on Boxing Day, 1910 with a production of the pantomime Jack and Jill.

The Village

Previous Page:
The spectacular view you get of the City of London from Marryat Road.

This Page: Lingfield and Homefield Roads in spring.

To celebrate this year's Jubilee, street parties were held all over the country. The weather wasn't that kind but that didn't dampen the spirits of Wimbledon folk; here the residents of Kenilworth Road enjoy themselves.

RIDGWAY
SW19 merton

The Top Four Pictures: Denmark Road, off the Ridgway, has some lovely houses with some excellent features. Also in the street is the home of The Belgrave Harriers (top right), one of London's more famous running clubs. Started in 1887, they took their name from the fact that its first headquarters were in Belgravia.

Bottom Left: The Argyle Estate, off Glen Albyn Road.

Bottom Right: Parkside Hospital is a private hospital and opened in 1983. There is a particularly fine conifer tree in its car park.

Queen Alexandra's Court, off St Mary's Road.
This little oasis of calm is home to 76 special ladies.
Founded in 1899 by Sir James Gildea, the founder
of what is now SSAFA Forces Help. When opened,
its main purpose was to provide accommodation for
ladies in reduced circumstances. Today it is a lovely
place with some beautiful gardens.

Thank you to Sarah Evans, the office manager, for letting me take some pictures.

Opposite: Stag Lodge was built in 1850 and marked the entrance to Earl Spencer's estate. One of his gardeners lived in the lodge, and there was once a gate here through which visitors could pass to get to the Manor House.

Right: Common West Side.

Below: The Common in winter.

South Wimbledon

Left: Several roads in South Wimbledon have connections with Lord Nelson whose estate covered this area. He moved to the house, Merton Place, in 1801 and lived here for just four years before his death at Trafalgar. As well as roads, there are many other references to Nelson in the area, including the hospital on the Kingston Road, the Trafalgar and Nelson Pubs plus a memorial garden, off High Path near Morden Road.

Far Left: The Gooseberry Bush café; besides their excellent home-made cakes they are also the only establishment of this type that I know that has a bike shed, with a roof and everything – well done them.

Bottom Left: South Wimbledon Station.

Bottom Right: The small triangular tract of land opposite Pizza Euforia, called Merton Rush, was saved recently from development by a local campaign, supported by many of the shops. Historically, the Rush was the centre of the old village.

Opposite: The Wimbledon Public Baths and Leisure Centre, Latimer Road, off The Broadway.

Pubs

Left: The Rose & Crown is Wimbledon's oldest pub, dating back to around 1650. The poets Leigh Hunt and Algernon Swinburne both drank here.

Top Right: The Alexandra was built in 1865 and was named after Queen Alexandra of Denmark, who married the Prince of Wales (later Edward VII) in 1863.

Bottom Right: The Sultan in Deburgh Road is a favourite with real ale drinkers and is the only Hop Back pub in London. The building dates from the 1930s.

89

Left: The Fox and Grapes started as The Union in 1838. It was used as a changing room for Old Centrals football team who played on the Common and eventually became Wimbledon FC. In 2011, it became a fine gastropub.

Right: In the 18th century the Crooked Billet pub was at the other end of the road known as Crooked Billet. It has been on the present site since the 1830s.

Far Left: There has been a pub on the site of the Dog & Fox for 500 years. It was originally known as The Sign of My Lord's Arms. The present building has been there since 1869.

Left: Berties Bar in Hartfield Road.

Bottom Left: The Prince of Wales in Hartfield Road.

Bottom Right: All Bar One in Wimbledon Hill Road.

Left: The Hand in Hand started as a bakery in 1865 and sold beer as a sideline. The pub was owned by the Holland family from then right up until it became a Young's pub in 1974.

Bottom Left: The Swan has been in the Ridgway since the 1850s and ran a horse and carriage service to Wimbledon station. The stables are still there today.

Top Opposite: Although the present building is relatively modern there has been a White Hart Inn here for over 300 years. It was here that Lord Nelson's estate was auctioned off in 1823. The tram runs past here on its way to New Addington (see page 2 for a picture of the tram).

Churches

Left: Christ Church, in West Wimbledon on the corner of Cottenham Park Road, was designed by Samuel Teulon and opened in 1859 and was intended as a chapel-of-ease to the parish church of St Mary's.

This Page: Holy Trinity church in Wimbledon Broadway celebrates its 150th anniversary in December 2012, and gave its name to nearby Trinity Road. Along with Christ Church, this church was intended as a chapel-of-ease to the parish church of St Mary's in the village.

This Page: The original St Mary's church on this site was mentioned in the Domesday Book, but the present building only dates back to 1843. Amongst the great and the good buried within the church yard are some members of the Watney family, who lived locally and Sir Joseph William Bazalgette, the famous engineer responsible for the London sewage system built in the late 1800s.

Opposite: The nave of the Sacred Heart church, on Edge Hill, was built in 1887 but the rest of the church was not completed until 1901.

Left: The Buddhapadipa Temple in Calonne Road was opened in 1980 and stands in four acres of grounds. It was the first Thai Buddhist temple to open in the UK.

Bottom Left: Local Roman Catholics had been worshipping at St Mary's school since 1882 and so St Winefride's church was built at Latimer Road in 1905.

Bottom Right: The Trinity United Reform Church in Mansel Road, as viewed from inside Wimbledon High School, opened in 1891 but since 1884 worshippers had been using the Drill Hall in St George's Road prior to the church being built.

Opposite Page: Emmanuel church in the Ridgway was built in 1888 when some of the congregation of St Mary's became dissatisfied with the way the church was being run under Canon Haygarth.

Bottom Right Opposite: Lucy and Will tie the knot at Emmanuel church in summer 2012.

Wimbledon Cemetery

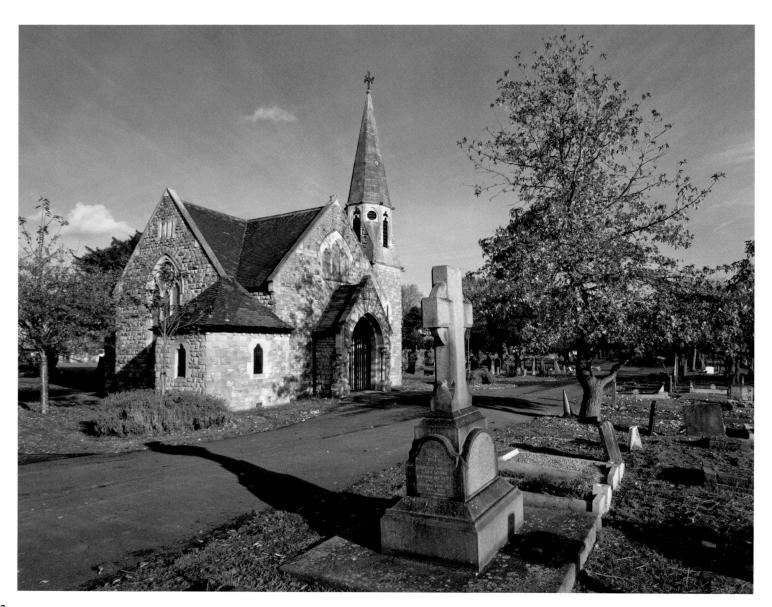

Schools

Page Opposite: Wimbledon Chase Primary School, off Merton Hall Road, can trace its history back to 1907 when a school for ninety young ladies was opened in Gladstone Road. In 1924, as the school grew bigger, a new school was built in Merton Hall Road on a site that had been a meeting place for staghounds in Tudor times. Now a primary school for children aged 3 to 11 years, they have some spectacular grounds.

Below: Dundonald Primary School, off Dundonald Road, was opened in 1894 and as can be seen still occupies its original Victorian building, which is impressive. Fully adapted on the inside for contemporary use, the school regularly uses the beautiful park that surrounds it on three sides (see page 159).

King's College School, overlooking Wimbledon Common, is an independent day school for boys aged 7–18 and girls aged 16–18. Founded in 1829 by Royal Charter, King's began life in the Strand and moved to Wimbledon in 1897. Its original school buildings date from this time and are surrounded by nearly twenty acres of sports pitches and laid-out gardens. King's is one of the top academic schools in the country and has over 1,300 pupils.

Ricards Lodge High School is hidden away behind a row of trees off Leopold Road, and boasts some wonderful grounds with facilities to match. Whilst excavating recently for a new all weather court, the school was surprised to find an old tunnel, apparently there to serve the Lord of the Manor, Earl Spencer.

The Study Preparatory School in Camp View on the common was established in 1893 by local governess, Miss Sidford, who started a small school in the house of Sir Arthur and Lady Holland in Wimbledon. A day school for girls aged 4 to 11, they also occupy another location at Spencer House in Peek Crescent, off Marryat Road.

Wimbledon College is a Roman Catholic voluntary-aided comprehensive school for boys aged 11 to 18 and founded in 1892 by the Jesuits, who still run the school. Situated in Edge Hill, it was originally in Darlaston Road.

Wimbledon High School is an independent school for girls aged 4 to 18 and was founded on its current location, the corner of Wimbledon Hill Road and Mansel Road, in 1880. From modest beginnings, the school is now considered to be one of London's very best. In a colourful history, the school survived a fire in 1917 and has a special association with the local tennis championships, as they took over the All England Club's original site in Nursery Road, where they play their sport.

Wimbledon Common

The common is perhaps the one feature of Wimbledon that makes it unique, desirable and special. In the 1860s the Lord of the Manor, Earl Spencer was planning to enclose the common as a public park, knock down the windmill and build himself a manor house in its place and to sell off Putney Heath for housing. Happily, a group of local people had other ideas and saved the common and heath for future generations. The Wimbledon and Putney Commons act received the royal assent in 1871 and the conservators group was formed.

Over the centuries the common has been used for duelling, prize fighting, horse racing, military manoeuvres and parades, sports, fairs, and many other activities. The forerunners of the FA cup-winning Wimbledon football club started on the common, Wimbledon Rugby Club, one of the earliest in the country, held their first matches here, and London Scottish, one of the oldest golf clubs in the country is based at the windmill. The common was also one of the earliest venues for cross-country running, ice skating, and many other sports. The National Rifle Association held its annual meetings here from 1860–1889, an event that made Wimbledon famous before the tennis started here.

To do the common justice a whole book would be needed to describe its history, its importance to the life of Wimbledon, its wildlife etc, but suffice to say that its importance lives on as a place of recreation, from horse-riding, to running, to cycling, to the annual village fair, to wildlife walks, rambles, bird-spotting, visiting the windmill, sketching, picnicking, or just finding a haven of peace away from the London traffic. We have a lot to thank those conservators for.

The Windmill

The windmill has been here since 1813 and is the last hollow-post mill in the country.

Right: The Windmill Café boasts that it is open every day bar Christmas Day. I have not been around to verify this but there is no doubt it is a very popular place with all those that visit the common.

Far Right: Each summer the Wimbledon and Putney Conservators, who control the common in both areas, hold an open day.

Rushmere Pond

Rushmere pond, on the Common, is so-called because the water was once surrounded by rushes, which were used by villagers in their primitive dwellings.

Opposite: Fun in the snow, February 2012.

Right: Egyptian Geese in the fog.

Left: Each summer a fair comes to the common but not always in the company of a Heron.

Right and Far Right: Family of Canada Geese.

The Village Fair

The Village Fair, held on the common every summer is sponsored by, amongst others, local estate agent Robert Holmes.

The Common

Bottom Left and Right:
Located outside the Windmill Museum is an old mill wheel from Canterbury. The museum, founded in 1976, is run by a charitable trust and is open on weekends from March to October.

Left: The path beside the Common Southside.

Below: Fly Agaric toadstools.

Above Left: A Great Spotted Woodpecker feeding its young down by Queensmere.

Above Right: Wimbledon Common.

Right: Haymaking in late summer up by the windmill.

The common is a wonderful place for horses and given the sheer size of the common, it is also the usual method by which the Rangers that patrol the common use to get around. The Rangers are employed by the Wimbledon and Putney Conservators, which is the body that has overall control of the commons.

Autumn Colours: The woods beside the Windmill (above) always have a wonderful display in autumn, as do the lime trees on the common up by Rushmere Pond (right).

Left: Bluegate Pond, near Parkside, March 2010. Despite all the rain in 2012, the pond is unfortunately almost dry, as are others on the Common.

Left: For a few years up until 2010, some people unknown used to dress a small conifer up by the Windmill at Christmas time (beside the path leading away from the Windmill towards Putney).

Bottom: One of the trees in winter by Queensmere.

Right and Overleaf: The line of trees beside the road leading to the Windmill.

Queensmere

Queensmere, near the Windmill, was artificially created in 1897 to celebrate the Diamond Jubilee of Queen Victoria.

After a few barren years, ever since the Rangers erected a couple of floating rafts in 2010 the pair of swans that inhabit Queensmere have bred successfully each year. When very young the cygnets need somewhere safe and warm to return at night and the rafts fit the bill perfectly.

Far Left: Quite a rare sight, a young Coot up on its mother's back.

Bottom Far Left: Grey Heron resting on one of the floating rafts.

Bottom Right: Canada Gosling.

Opposite: One of the Rangers talking to visitors to the Common.

Overleaf: The colours around Queensmere in autumn can be spectacular.

Golf Courses

There are three golf courses on Wimbledon Common: The London Scottish, based at the windmill, which is the third oldest in the country, the Wimbledon Common Golf Club, and the Royal Wimbledon Golf Club near Caesar's Camp.

This Page:
The London Scottish.

Above Left and Far Left:
Wimbledon Common beside Camp View.

Left and Opposite:
The Royal Wimbledon Golf Club, as with The London Scottish, is one of the oldest clubs in the country. Rich in tradition, the club continues to invest in its facilities and as recently as four years ago spent over £1m in completely redeveloping their clubhouse (see opposite).

Parks and Gardens

In addition to the common and Wimbledon Park we have a host of other parks and gardens in Wimbledon ranging from postage stamp plots tucked away off side streets to the rather exotic Cannizaro Park.

Cannizaro gets its name from the Duke of Cannizaro, a Sicilian nobleman who married a Scottish heiress and Cannizaro house was the venue for many parties attended by Prime Minister William Pitt in the early 1800s. The grounds were opened as a public park in 1948 and have been used for open-air theatre and sculpture exhibitions. There is a wide variety of interesting plants and some beautiful walks.

Dundonald recreation ground is a park in all but name but is unfortunately currently under threat of being built on with an extension of Dundonald school. The bowling green has already been closed but at the moment the park is still well-used and well-loved by local people.

The pretty Holland Gardens, which was once a field owned by local resident Sir Arthur Holland, was given to the council for use as a public park in 1929.

John Innes park was originally the garden of John Innes, the man whose name is known to gardeners everywhere and whose money went to establish the John Innes plant research centre in Norwich. Innes stipulated in his will that his garden be used as a public park and that it should contain, among other things, a bandstand, tennis courts and croquet lawn, all of which survive and are still used today.

It would be difficult to be anywhere in Wimbledon that wasn't a short walk from an open space, and in a city as large and populous as London that is truly remarkable.

2012 was a good year for the parks and gardens of Merton, as they won five Green Flag's, which is a national award given to the best public parks and green spaces. And I'm pleased to say that three of them are covered here in this book, Dundonald Recreation Ground, John Innes Park and South Park Gardens. I love green spaces and Merton Council should be congratulated, as five awards was one more than they achieved last year. For more information on the Green Flag Awards and to discover the other two in Merton please visit www.greenflagaward.org.uk

Previous Page: Dundonald Recreation Ground.

This Page: Raynes Park Recreation Ground in West Wimbledon with its lovely pavilion, sadly in need of a bit of TLC.

Opposite: Holland Gardens in West Wimbledon was once a field owned by local resident Sir Arthur Holland, given to the council for use as a public park in 1929.

Opposite: South Park Gardens
off Trinity Road.

This Page: Haydons Park Recreation
Ground off Quick's Road.

John Innes Park

John Innes park was originally the garden of John Innes, the man whose name is known to gardeners everywhere and whose money went to establish the John Innes plant research centre in Norwich. Innes stipulated in his will that his garden be used as a public park and that it should contain, among other things, a bandstand, tennis courts and croquet lawn, all of which survive and are still used today.

Other books by Andrew Wilson from the Wild series

WILD ABOUT KEW
Published 2011

WILD ABOUT BARNES
Second edition published 2012

WILD ABOUT PUTNEY
Published 2012

WILD IN THE CITY
Published 2009

THE WILD SERIES IS AVAILABLE TO BUY AT ALL GOOD BOOK STORES INCLUDING BARNES, KEW AND SHEEN BOOKSHOPS, WIMBLEDON BOOKS AND MUSIC AND ALL BRANCHES OF WATERSTONES.

Follow Andrew on Twitter: @andrewpics

Andrew uses Canon Camera equipment

WILD ABOUT THE THAMES
Published 2010

First Edition – ©Unity Print and Publishing Limited 2012

Designed by Ball Design Consultancy. *www.balldesignconsultancy.com*

Printed by Headley Brothers of Ashford, Kent. *www.headley.co.uk*

Bound by Green Street Bindery of Oxford. *www.maltbysbookbinders.com*

Colour Management by Paul Sherfield of The Missing Horse Consultancy. *www.missinghorsecons.co.uk*

Published by Unity Print and Publishing Limited, 18 Dungarvan Avenue, London SW15 5QU

Tel: +44 (0)20 8487 2199
aw@unity-publishing.co.uk
www.unity-publishing.co.uk